Jack Gets Grounded

Paul L Hardwicke

Poems by Pill

Published by

Paul L Hardwicke

Copyright © 2015

Paul L Hardwicke

JACK GETS GROUNDED

Jack was in his bedroom

He was grounded for being naughty

He was sent there by his dad

What does he know, he's over forty?

He only pulled his sister's hair

And set her hamster free

Then was snitched on by his mum

Who should know better at thirty three?

Although my sister is only six

Her hair got in my eyes

I only moved it out the way

When she let out her cries

And as regards to the hamster

I know this sounds quite weak

But I did it as a surprise for her

As she likes to play hide and seek

So now I sit here grounded

There's nothing I can do

The computer is in the study

And my games console too

I haven't any books to read

For games you need more than one

So I will have to sit here very bored

I could bounce on the bed for fun

I can hear my friends outside my house

On bikes and skateboards too

I can hear them laughing and joking

I'm here like a caged animal in the zoo

Now it's gone very quiet

They are going home for tea

They'll have big smiles on their faces

Not like sad old me

What's that noise I'm hearing?

I bet its Zack, to get my attention

Throwing stones at my window

To tell me news while I'm in detention

I better go and have a look

At least I can have a chat

And maybe watch them playing cricket

Using a table leg as a bat

On drawing back the curtains

The street is bare I see

Not a single mate was in sight

My minds playing tricks with me

But what's that on the window sill

A dirty crumpled puppet

Laying soiled and in a heap

It looks a proper Muppet

Should I bring it in I thought

And throw it around the room

At least it's something new to do

Or I could use it as a broom

So I opened up the window

And picked up the crumpled mess

It was a cross between Pinocchio

And a doll in fancy dress

Cobwebs on its head

It looked a proper disgrace

Half a snail shell on its foot

And sand all over its face

But on giving it closer inspection

I could see it wasn't a puppet

I thought I saw strings attached

And looked more like, little Miss Muffet

Then I noticed something else

For what I thought was strings

Was more like an old net curtain?

In fact it was wearing wings

It must be some kind of fairy doll

With long blonde straggly hair

Landing on my window sill

Thrown in the air without a care

Perhaps if I straighten up the wings

I could make it fly

Flying it around the room

Might not work, but I can try

Slowly I stretched out the wings

There were 4 they looked quite neat

They folded up when I let them go

And removed the snail shell from its feet

After having another thought

Working out what to do?

Using some straws and super glue

Or a stick a nail and a screw

I will have to search my bedroom

And see what I can find

It will be harder than I thought

This will tax my mind

So I started to have a rummage

Sorting through all my goods

A conker a marble 2 dead flies

That won't get me out of the woods

I found a couple of big blue straws

Stuck in a sausage with batter

That will do just nicely I think

I don't think the grease will matter

Now I need a piece of string

There's nothing on the conker

But there's a piece in some old chocolate

When I tried to be Willy Wonka

Now I need a screw

From the wardrobe I will pry

If it collapses during the night

I'll blame it on dads DIY

Take the picture off the wall

Remove the nail, its not to long

Then use my old school ruler

For the wood, that's very strong

Now I have all the bits I need

It should not take too long

But I better give it a clean-up first

It has an awful pong

So off I go to the bathroom

To fetch a flannel and water

Shampoo, soap and deodorant

Should make the job much shorter

Returning from the bathroom

I put the things by the side of the bed

In case mum or dad come in

If they catch me then I'm dead

Then when I was ready to start

I turned to pick up Trong

I thought of that name in the bathroom

And it rhymes with pong

But when I went to pick it up

It was no longer there

I bet my sister's taken it

While in the bathroom, she wouldn't care

So I stormed into her bedroom

But, she was not there

Curtains open bed still made

And teddy sitting on the chair

She must have taken it downstairs

While I wasn't looking

So I shouted "have you been in my room"

Mum said no she's helping me do the cooking

So I went back in my room

I think I'm off my head

Or is it that I didn't look

It may have fallen off the bed

So down on my hands and knees

To search through all the junk

I should clean it up one day

And put it in the trunk

Well it's not beside the bed

Perhaps it could be under

I did come rushing in the room

After shouting out like thunder

Well there it is, there is Trong

Underneath the bed

I think I must have kicked him there

While going off my head

I pulled him out and dusted him

Then placed him on his back

Now to start the clean up

I'm good I have the knack

So I put the flannel in the water

And rubbed the soap to a lather

This is something I don't normally do

According to my father

But just as I was ready

I thought I heard a groan

I bet it's my horrible sister

All she does is moan

Then I heard the noise again

It's not my sister the brat

She squeals and squeals and squeals and squeals

She's sounds like a strangled cat

I was shocked when I turned around

And much to my surprise

There was Trong sitting up

With tears running down his eyes

I thought he must be drying out

And sat up as he shrunk

And the tears were only water

But he did still smell like a skunk

Then I saw his arm move

And a twitch came from the other

I throw myself off the bed

And nearly shouted for my mother

I think I must be seeing things

It's a bit dim in the house

I pulled myself together

And thought inside there must be a mouse

As I got a little closer

And feeling scared as well

A little hand brushed away a tear

It's real now I could tell

Now I don't know what to do

I'm alone inside my room

With I just don't know what!

That I was going to groom

Now how do I deal with this?

Do I try to talk to Trong?

I bet he has a different name

The one I made up, will be wrong

Then came my worst nightmare

He turned and spoke to me

How come I'm sitting on a bed?

And how come you can see me

I'm supposed to be invisible

To all the girls and boys

They only see me in their mind

When playing with dolls and toys

I must have upset my magic

I remember the sound of a train

It made me jump; I went down with a bump

And fell down a smelly old drain

When I got out I tried to fly

And that was rather erratic

I aimed for hole in your roof

So I could clean myself up in your attic

But that is all I remember

Perhaps you can fill me in

And enlighten me on my demise

My head sounds like a stone in a tin

Well I said I'll let you know

All I can, to help you out

But I think that I'm still dreaming

And still I have a bit of doubt

Perhaps if you give me a pinch

I'll know I'm not in a dream

Then I won't wake with a shake and shiver

And let out a big scary scream

I'll pop down and get some milk

I know that I can risk it

If your still here when I get back

You can share a ginger biscuit

Before I go down the stairs

By the bed there's some water in a bowl

A soap and flannel are next to it

You can start washing, and dry on the towel

So I nipped down the stairs

And to mum, I started to speak

May I have some biscuits and milk please?

I'm sorry I made my sister squeak

So I went back up to my room

Expecting no little people to see

I must be awake, I even got cake

My mum was really pleased with me

I returned back to my bedroom

With a wide smile on my face

But on the bed with foam on his head was Trong

My heart started to race

Well now I know you're real

So what am I to do?

First we better get you clean

And then we'll feed you too

Would you like to change your clothes?

I have some action man suits

I even have some little socks

And a pair of commando boots

Trong said that would be nice

I will get mine cleaned when I get home

We have a super little laundry

Run by a big purple gnome

Jack said that is funny

I thought gnomes were concrete or plastic

Only the ones in your garden

The real ones are really fantastic

They run all the shops and restaurants

And look after all our needs

While us fairies fly round the world

Doing all the good deeds

You have shops and restaurants?

Yes said Trong they're great

We eat leaves, flowers and berries

On an upside down mushrooms as plate

I'm sorry but I gave you a name

When I thought you were not real

I called you Trong, because it rhymed with pong

That's ok, it's no big deal

In fact I rather like it

It rolls off the tongue with ease

And you couldn't use my real one

As it's the sound of leaves falling off trees

So carry on and call me Trong

What's yours, my name is Jack

I was named after my granddad

Who lives in the house around the back?

We fairies remember Mary his wife

In the garden she liked to talk to us

She waved goodbye every day

When she went down town on the bus

We all felt very sad and lost

The day that Mary died

We all went to her funeral

And cried and cried and cried

We don't have many grownups who believe in us

And leave us food and drink

All those adult none believers

We think they really stink

Well I believe in you now said jack

And you seem so good

It looks as if you care for people

Even one's nobody else would

We never stop believing said Trong

Children seem to forget us with age

As some forget others start to believe

It's just like turning a new page

Do all fairies die said Jack?

No we just fade away

When 100 children stop believing

One of us will disappear that day

But don't think it's bad or sad

And it's just too hard to explain

We do not die we just say goodbye

And go away on the forgotten fairy train

But that's not the end of us

And our future is not lost

We wait and wait and wait and wait

In the land of old Jack Frost

And when 100 children believe in us again

We return once more on the train

To look after all those who believe

And do our good deeds once again

Well I feel a lot better now

Just to hear the words you say

Knowing that if you disappear

You'll be returning once again one day

Well you look a lot better now

You are so nice and clean

Dressed up as an action man

Now you look good enough to be seen

But that is a little ironic

As us humans cannot see

But if they could

You could hide camouflaged in a big tree

The biscuit and milk was lovely

I'm feeling a lot better now

I can fly all the way home now

I won't have to stop to drink milk from a cow

It's been very nice to meet you Jack

And you have been very kind

I would like to do something in return

And I have something in mind

Jacks mind started to daydream

Whatever can it be?

Perhaps I'll get a magic wish

And a millionaire I will be

No said Trong it's not that

Hey can you read my mind

Yes said Trong. I must be getting strong

Are my wings turning blue behind?

Only very pale blue

Will they go real dark?

The same colour as the swings

Down at your local park

Is there anything else said Jack

That will change as you get stronger

My skin will turn green like a runner bean

And my ears will get pointed and longer

Then my hair will go all pink

And look like it's covered in down

No I'm only kidding

It just turns mousey brown

I think that you are funny Trong

Are all the fairies funny, Hee! Hee!

Yes said Trong when you come along

You will be able to see

When I come along said Jack

What do you think your saying?

I bet you're being funny again

And with me you're only playing

No said Trong I mean come along

With me to fairy land

It's my treat for being so sweet

I think you are really grand

But I'm just a little boy

I know that I can't fly

I've jumped up and down on my bed

And when I land it makes me cry

I've banged my leg and my head

With bruises all over me

And mum has to put ointment on

It's smelly that TCP

Now I think you are pulling my leg

And possibly the other one too

This is just a joke again

Tell me is it really true

Yes said Trong I mean come along

I am telling you the truth

We can fly in the sky right up high

And you can sit on the roof

But I haven't any wings

And I'm really big

And if I landed on a tree

I'll need a branch to sit on, not a twig

I'd need wings as big as a jumbo jet

And an engine on my back

I'm too young for a pilot's license

That's one thing that I lack

And then what about mum and dad

They'll miss me and my tricks

I have to have my dinner soon

It's always ready at half past six

Then my sister will want to play with me

Before she goes to bed

And I'll know you are upstairs

And my face will go all red

You don't have to worry

For when my magic's back

You will see that I can do anything

That's no problem Jack

I can shrink you down to my size

And you'll be green and hairy

The only little problem is

We'll have to change your name to Mary

That's not fair because I'm a boy

Can't I keep my name?

Of course you can do not fear

I'm just playing a little game

You'll have wings just like me

And be invisible too

I'll take you off to fairy land

It'll be special just for you

We can do this for children

Who do special things for us?

And show them what the fairies do

For helping and not making a fuss

Your wings are getting darker now

And your skin is turning green

Your wings will soon be the colour of the swings

And your skin's like a runner bean

I know said Trong it won't be long

I can feel magic getting stronger

My hair's gone brown

And I can feel my ears getting longer

How long will we be away?

Mum and dad will miss me I know

That's ok jack when we get back

For them the time would go slow

We can go on our trip

And be away for hours

But when we return it will be seconds for them

As that's within my powers

Because we live forever

We do not use your time

We use the frogs in the pond

And how many are covered with slime

I bet you're being funny again

I know its fun said Trong

But as we live for ever

Your time would be too long

I think your magic is back now

I can't see you anymore

No it's not quite ready Jack

When you turned I jumped on the floor

I have to pack my clothes away

So I can carry them home

You know where I have to take them

Yes the big blue gnome

Trong jumped back on the bed

Nearly all his colour was back

My clothes are in my pocket

My magic is on track

I can't see your clothes said Jack

Did you leave them on the floor?

No, the pockets are magic to

I can fit in lots more

In one I could put an elephant

And in another a kangaroo

In fact if I wanted to

I could fill them with a whole Zoo

I think your being funny again

No said Trong that's right

In one I could put the day time

And in the other one, the night

You see they have to be magic

So big it's almost scary

Can you imagine how big the pockets would be?

On the little tooth fairy

She has to carry all the money

And all those teeth she has to collect

If she drove around in an artic

The children wouldn't give her respect

Everything here is normal size

Where I live everything's not

I could pick up your whole house

And put in a little tea pot

So what are your thoughts now Jack

Are you coming along with me?

Now you know that you will be safe

And you will be back in time for your tea

I think it will be great said Jack

Yes of course I'de love to come

Seeing all those magical things

Rather than sit here getting a numb bum

Put one of those biscuits in your pocket

You can use it as your in-flight meal

As you're not used to flying

And on landing you don't have a wheel

Do you have an airport?

And a tower to guide you in

No said Trong just a pond with a pong

And a very big rusty old tin

There is an old ginger moggy

With a scented candle he sniffs by his side

We call him Catwick Air Snort

He tries to catch us, but we always hide

I think you are nearly ready said Jack

You are starting to disappear

I know said Trong it won't be long

But me, you will still be able to hear

And then when I am completely gone

My magic I will use on you

And when you are down to my size

You will see my wings really beep blue

Well as Trong vanished from sight

And Jack eyes started to stream

I bet this is't real and I'll let out a squeal

As I wake from a very strange dream

Nothing has happened I'm still the same size

And hear my mum on the stairs

She's coming for me its dinner time see

I've Sheppard's pie followed by pears

She's coming up to my room

I know the last step has a squeak

The knob turns on the door

I was dreaming my life is so bleak

Hello said Trong you did come along

Jack said, you cut that real fine

With mum's hand on the door

I thought I was still in dream time

So you still had your doubts

About all what's gone on

I do understand now take my hand

And both of us will be gone

Can I look into the mirror first said jack?

I want to see how I look

Of course said Trong

While you do, I'll check my magic book

Jack looked in the glass in amazement

Then he fell down on his bum

He had a feel, the wings were real

They were pink just like bubble gum

Why are my wings all pink?

I thought like yours, they would be blue

That's always's planned its set up in hand

So all fairies know you're a visitor to

I don't know how to fly said Jack

Don't worry the magic will work?

When you take off you will have a small cough

And you will feel a bit of a jerk

Jack was concerned as his head turned

Remembering his mum at the door

Why has she not come in he thought?

It's the magic time, as I said before

It's now time Jack, that we departed

So climb up here with me on the sill

We will take off, don't forget the cough

Do I need a travel sickness pill?

You'll be alright and traveling by night

You will see all the houses lit up

But do not despair when we get there

We'll have nectar in a big buttercup

I'll take you over the top of your school

And then we'll fly past the park

I bet you shiver when you see the river

Everything lovely when you fly in the dark

So up on the sill stood Jack and Trong

This is still hard to believe

I'm just a boy who thinks he will fly

Am I just being naive?

If I just jump will I go down with a bump?

And end up flat on the floor

No said Trong just jump along

And up into the air we will sore

Jack let out a squeal, this can't be real

I'll crash and that's a bet

He didn't't fall long as he jumped off with Trong

He was flying like a jumbo jet

Cor! This is great, you're such a mate

This is the best thing that's happened to me

Just concentrate or your best mate

Will be scraping you off that oak tree

Sorry said Jack I had to look back

My house looks so different from here

There's my lost ball in the gutter

And a top from dads bottle of beer

I'm having real fun and it's only begun

And I know I won't be home late

And them with a dive past a bee hive

Trong flew us right through the park gate

Then with a whoosh and whiz

We flew past a big bat

Not strange so you think

But he was wearing a top hat

He reminds me of count Dracula

A scary that I see on the telly

Maybe said Jack but don't follow him back

His home is awfully smelly

Then Trong took me to my school

It looked strange from up in the air

We flew round and round and up and down

It's a pity that no one is there

And up in that tree is a squirrel you see

He lives there in a dray

I know said Jack when we turn our back

He steals our lunch when we go out to play

Now we'll go down to the river

We'll swoop really low down

And scare the gnats and fireflies

And make the gold lights go brown

You really have fun when you're flying

I know Jack that's how we are

But you have to be very careful

One day I flew into a jar

I was chasing a jackdaw in summer

His feathers were shiny and black

The sun shone off his wing into my eyes

And I crashed in the jar on my back

I think you are a little bit clumsy

How many accidents have you had?

I'm not sure said Trong, but the list is long

In fact I'm very bad

Now you have to tell me

I hope we will be alright

Yes said Trong we won't be long

Chill out and enjoy the flight

I am said jack I never thought

I would ever fly by myself

As I said I used to jump on the bed

And often hit my head on the shelf

I think that you are as clumsy as me

Said Trong to Jack we are a pair

But my hair is brown and wings are blue

Yours are pink and so is your hair

I've got pink hair are you sure?

I think you're talking junk

I'm not said Trong it's spiky and long

Oh no! I'll look like a punk

To you, you do but not to us

As you will soon find out

We are nearly there and today is the fair

I bet you won't stick out

Having a fair I bet that's a joke

No said Trong it's true

Every month on a full moon

There will be lots of things to do

So way up high in the woods they flew

At night time, just watch out for trees

During the day the trees are ok

But you have to watch out for the bees

Do you ever come to the woods Jack?

Yes sometimes with mum and dad

We look for chestnuts to roast at home

If we find none, dad gets real mad

We eat lots of chestnuts

Some for the winter we store

We give them to the silly squirrels

They can't dig up theirs it makes their feet sore

Sometimes we look for Pine cones

For Christmas mum paints them gold

Then sticks them on a rustic log

She's good, some of them she's sold

We also pick lots of holly

We make a wreath, to hang on the door

Its looks good for all the carol singers

Who get 50p, if they sing 2 songs or more?

Can you see the clearing ahead said Trong?

Soon you will hear all the noise

All lit up by bugs in buttercups

They are glow worms and fireflies

Yes said Jack I can see it now

It really does look pretty good

And no one knows it's here at all

Deep inside the wood

Yes said Trong it's a secret

And no one can ever see

Only very special humans

Who come with other fairies or me?

So let's go down and see the sights

And you can meet all of my friends

Then we'll go on all the rides

And stay here till the fair ends

Why do you have the fair each month?

Jack said with a bit of a cough

Well said Trong we work so hard and long

It's the only day that we get off

So Trong and Jack landed, with a bit of a bump

By a big crowd of his mates, who looked scary?

Hi said Trong I brought a human along

Pink wings pink hair, do we call him Mary

My name is Jack, I mentioned that

About the pink and the name

I wanted Blue and green skin like you

I knew Trong was playing game

I see you have a new name said Russell

Who was named after a leaf in the breeze?

Yes said Trong just play along

I didn't't tell him my name was sneeze

Being funny again said jack to Trong

Don't worry we all play these games

Just call all of us Trong

And the magic will convert all our names

So when you say Trong to Russell

He will only hear Russell you see

The same goes for Flumble and Rumble

And Huffle, Shuffle and tee

Well I'm happy with that, said Jack

As long as you all understand

So can we all go play on the fair

Jack, now you can let go of my hand

So Jack asked Trong what shell we go on

And Trong said ask Trong, and Trong put his head

down and hid

So Trong asked Trong did you ask Trong and Trong

said I thought I just did

Very funny said Jack to the Trongs

Are we going on all the rides?

Yes we will, and to start with a thrill

We'll go on the caterpillar slides

When we got there I stopped to stare

Such a wonderful sight for my eyes to see

The biggest beautiful caterpillar

From the top of an old oak tree

It was blue and green and yellow and red

With diamonds and emeralds to

And lights of every colour

Something my friends would just love to do

We all flew up to the top of the tree

And got in the queue waiting there

Then when it was my turn to go down

You had to sit a small rocking chair

I sat in the chair, without even a care

And started to go down the slide

The chair was rocking, my knees were knocking

I knew it would be a great ride

But all the fun had only just begun

As the caterpillar arched up its back

So as I started down I laughed like a clown

Was I scared, well my wings turned to black

I carried on going toing and frowing

Then upside down on the chair

Then with a bump in my throat a lump

I landed with multi coloured hair

Did you find that ride shocking said Trong?

A little I said with a stutter

That's good said Trong, so come along

Next is the butterfly flutter

That sounds a bit milder I thought to myself

Butterflies are very gentle in flight

I kept telling myself this

And I knew, I would be quite alright

Look up there Jack, in the sky o so black

Were butterflies with colours so bright?

Hanging on threads of silver and gold

In contrast to the darkness of night

I want the white one, said Jack to the Trong's

It doesn't matter which one you pick

They'll all change colours when on the ride

You'll go yellow and then you'll be sick

Stop being silly, said Jack to the Trongs

Butterflies are gentle and sweet

I know said Trong but these are not real

So don't have anything to eat

I know you're being silly again

And I won't believe you this time

I'm really going to enjoy this ride

Said Trong watch out for the slime

So up we all went into the sky

And sat on a butterfly of choice

Just hang on tight, you'll be alright

Said Jack, I know this will be nice

So rather like the chain chairs on our fairs

The butterflies slowly went round

A little bit faster a little bit higher

No need to scream or make a sound

This is fantastic like being on elastic

And the speed was not very fast

Then it got quicker and I felt much sicker

And then Trong came whizzing past

How did he do that?

His thread must have broke off his seat

I think he may crash and get a bash

Or hurt the soles of his feet

There's a bit of a nasty pong said Trong

Said Jack, I think it comes from the houses

No said Trong you have that one wrong

I'm sure it comes from your trousers

That's not nice I wasn't scared

Although it was very fast

My eyes did water and my hair stood on end

But I thought it was a blast

Well said Trong lets move along and go to the teasel

shy

It's like a coconut shy but with teasels instead

I can knock them off easy said jack

I don't think so in the bottom there's lead

Doing that is cheating said Jack

Yes but there's no prizes to win

It's only for fun and you get a blue bun

You can throw on the next stall at a tin

Everything here is strange said Jack

But very exciting as well

Are they racing frogs over there?

And candy floss I can smell

Would you like to go on the frogs said Trong?

And eat candy floss flavored with slime

I think I'll give that one a miss

And do the candyfloss another time

So over we went to the racing frogs

All the Trongs with candy floss in hand

At least I won't get covered in sticky goo

I bet they had that one planned

Thinking I was going to get one

And then hop around on a frog

They would laugh at me all pink and sticky

I would look like a pink fluffy hog

All the frogs looked the same

So I jumped on the one at the back

Holding on tight we hopped off into the night

It looked awfully scary and black

The hops were just little to start off

Then they got higher, higher

Down by the river and over a log

Mines fast I think he's a flyer

Then we went into a tunnel

The Trongs were screaming with glee

When I came out I let out a shout

I had pink candy floss all over me

I knew that was going to happen

They all laughed at the state I was in

But the candy floss did taste nice

And the Trongs were still making a din

How am I going to get this off?

It's nice but sticky as well

It won't be on to long said my mate Trong

He had something planned I could tell

So off we hopped gathering speed

I stared to shake and shiver

And with one last hop and a big plop

We all plunged into the river

I said you would not have it on long

I kept my promise you see

Yes said jack you certainly did

But all the fishes are nibbling me

Don't worry about the little ones

Candy floss is something they like

It's the frog you have to worry about

There the favorite food for the big pike

So wash off the candy floss quickly

And hop out onto the bank

Then we'll go back to the fair

And play pirates walking the plank

I suppose I'll get wet again

Not if you win the game

And you dress as a pirate

And choose a pirate name

So I cleaned off all the candy floss

Then we hopped off back to the fair

There were hundreds of pixies and fairies

And a leprechaun on an old rocking chair

So off we went to the pirate ship

And dressed in a costume of choice

I became captain black with one leg

And spoke in a very deep voice

So how do we play the game said Jack?

It's easy said Trong with a smile

You just swing out over the water

And try to land on the big crocodile

If you land on the croc said Trong

That's considered a win

If you miss all pirates hiss

Then it's the plank and you have to go in

That doesn't seem to bad said jack

And the croc is rather large

It will just like a little fly

Landing on a boat the size of a barge

Then one Trong went and then another

And both landed on the croc

It seems it's just getting the timing right

I'll count the seconds as I watch the clock

Then it was time for my mate Trong

And he nearly missed

He managed to hold on to its tail

All the Trongs nearly hissed

I thought I'de see him walk the plank

And get wet in the deep black lake

I want to hear them hiss and scream

When one of them made a mistake

Then it came to my turn

I had the timing down to a tee

I'll swing out over the water

And let go when I counted to three

Everyone will cheer and shout

As I land on its back with perfection

But just as I was ready to go

An elf jumped on the croc for an inspection

I think they had a little fault

But the elf will soon put that right

Said Trong it should not take too long

It happens about twice a night

Then the elf finished off his work

I swung out and counted to three

Then I let go I'll win I just know

But the croc disappeared from the sea

I should have known better

I should know I can't win

And with a big splash

Jack belly flopped in

As jack came back up to the surface

The hissing was loud in his ears

If Jack had been a big sissy

His eyes would be filled with tears

As Jack climbed out they started to shout

Jack thought I'll how I don't care

But that was never going to work

With limp wings and more pond weed than hair

Jack climbed back on the pirate ship

The hissing turned into cheers

You were just great and our best mate

And there's newts in both of your ears

Oh that's funny said jack to the Trongs

As he pulled some weed from his neck

He shook his head to remove the rest

And 2 newts run off down the deck

We said you had newts in your ears

I thought you were all being funny

It would have been if they were frogs

Or bees with pots of honey

Jack just smiled and said to the Trongs

Let's go off to the plank

I know that I will get wet again

Trong said on that I would not bank

What do you mean I won't get wet?

I will if I go in the drink

But this plank is not over water

More hundreds and thousands in blue, yellow and

pink

Being funny again said Jack

As he climbed on the board of fate

Then he walked to the end and looked down

Hundreds and thousands oh that's just great

Jack stood on the board just trembling

Not from the demise of his fate

It was the hundreds of pixies and fairies

The elves and goblins, Jack thought great

All of them shouting and hissing

Waiting for jack to go in

I'm going to be brave and give them a wave

As I dive in the multi coloured bin

Jack waved to the crowds as they all hissed

He bowed like a performer on stage

Put out his arms and dived in the air

As he landed his smiles turned to rage

Jack thought that he would be licking his lips

As he landed in the big tasty treat

But no hundreds and thousands

Just multi coloured maggots tickling his feet

Jack jumped out very quickly

But still had to give out a giggle

Between his toes and one up his nose

Were three maggots still having a wiggle?

Everyone cheered and shouted

As Jack tried to shake off the worms

I hope that I will be alright

And don't catch to many germs

Jack kicked his leg and a maggot flew off

The other flew from his toe to his knee

Along came a breeze Jack let out a sneeze

And a blue maggot flew up in a tree

The noise got louder and louder

As Jack looked like he was trying to dance

It may be fun for everyone

But Jack was just in a trance

The Trongs came down to join jack

And cheered and said he was great

We've have just the time for one more ride

Because it's getting quite late

I thought that your magic lasted forever

It does but we still have to work

But this one day a month is our bonus

It's like doing a job with a perk

What is a perk said jack to the Trongs?

Well let us see if we can explain one

It's like having a job with MacDonald's

You get a free burger in a bun

Now I understand said Jack

I know that you work hard day and night

To do all the special things for the children

To make the bad things turn out alright

So shall we go to the haunted log?

The ride is creepy and dark

It goes in the big hollow log

The one laying just outside the park

I don't mind I don't get scared

I've been on the ghost train you see

I think you'll be frightened on this one

When you are chased by a big angry bee

But its night time said Jack

And the bees are asleep in their hive

And when we go past very very fast

You will see their awake and alive

But this one is a little bit different

On this we only walk and run

That way it's much more scary

It's spooky and much more fun

So off we went to the big hollow log

To get ready for the last ride

This time I'm going to be really brave

And my eyes I will not hide

We all stood outside the log

And got in single file

Trong said you have to run very fast

Can you run a four minute mile?

I'll try and run as fast as I can

And keep up to all your speed

You'll have to run faster than that

You're up front you're in the lead

Thanks said jack that's very nice

So you shouldn't be last

And you have to remember

We've all done it in the past

So are you ready to run then Jack

Are you ready to be scared out of your pants?

And before you get out you'll scream and shout

And be covered with ants

Ready steady go said Trong

And jack ran into the log like a cat

He got a big cobweb in his face

On his head was a vampire bat

Jack screamed out I hate bats

As he pulled the cobweb from his face

At least there aren't any spiders

There is on your back so pick up the pace

Jack tried to run faster

But tripped up over his lace

All the Trong's landed on top of him

And there were rats all over the place

Jack struggled to get off the floor

And shake off all of his mates

Then hands came out of the walls

With jelly and custard on plates

As jack got ready to run again

A jelly hit him in the face

Jack slipped on some custard

Trong shouted do up your lace

Jack struggled to do up his lace

As more jelly run down his neck

He ran on the spot in the custard

And felt a bit of a wreck

Then his feet started to grip

And ran further into the log

As he went round the corner

He ran into a wet fog

I can't see in this fog said Jack

It's not fog said a voice from the rear

Its bubbles of slime made by frogs

Watch a tadpole don't get in your ear

Jack wanted to shout back to them

But the thought of a tadpole going in

Made him keep his mouth shut

With his hands covering up his grin

As he emerged from the bubbles

With spawn all down his nose

A thousand golden eyes whizzed about

Attached to flapping crows

Jack ducked and dived moved side to side

To try and avoid their wings

He never liked birds that much

Then found they were hanging on strings

Jack was feeling better now

Till an owl landed on his head

I bet it just a plastic one

As he felt his face go red

Then the owl gave a hoot

And Jack screamed out in surprise

It was real he let out a squeal

As a tear rolled from his eyes

His knees begun to knock

And his body started to shiver

He fell on his bum and went quite numb

He came over all a quiver

I must pull myself together

And get through this log of fright

I must be strong to carry on

I know I'll be alright

Jack stood up straight like superman

I'll be strong right to the end

Then a hitch, he ran into a witch

As he went dashing round a bend

The witch didn't say a word

Just pointed a finger, then flash

He felt a tingle all over his body

Like when he had a measles rash

Suddenly he could see in the dark

That's handy in this dark hollow hole

Not that handy said the witch

Look! You're a little furry mole

Jack squealed out, for a mole not loud

And tried to run real fast

The next second he was a little cat

After another electrifying blast

Jack gave out a little purr

And a small meow

He tried to scamper away from the witch

As another spark hit his bum ow

Now I'm back to normal

He let out a happy wail

The witch shouted out not quite yet

Look behind you, oh no I have a tail

It was a curly piggy one

It wiggled as he ran away

Just think of the fun your friends will have

When you go out to play

Jack didn't take any notice

He ran as fast as he could

I just have to get away from the witch

Or next time I'll be a piece of wood

Jack went round the corner

He run and run and run

Out of the log and into the night

It was scary but very good fun

Jack pulled himself together

And turned to wait for his mates

But there they were seated on the ground

Eating sandwiches and cakes off mushroom plates

Jack said that was very sneaky

How did you beat me here?

Well just before you reached the witch

There was a door saying exit here

Well thanks very much for telling me

May I have that cherry cake?

Only if you wiggle your piggy tail

Go on, give it a little shake

I thought that would disappear

How long will it take to go?

You will have to wait till winter

It will drop off in the snow

I can't wait that long said Jack

I have to go to school in the morning

But if you wiggle it in the class

It will stop your friends from yawning

Sit and eat your cherry cake

Then have a blackberry pie

It will make you wheeze then you'll sneeze

And your tail will fly into the sky

Jack gave a little smile

That would be a tall tail he said

I often pick blackberries for my mum

Her pies make my tongue go red

So Jack finished off his cherry cake

And his blackberry pie quite fast

He wheezed and sneezed and was very pleased

As his tail shot off with a blast

Jack said I feel better now

I can hold my head up high

Then he felt a slap on his back

As the tail crashed back from the sky

Trong said I think it likes you

You can keep it as a souvenir

No said jack you can take it back

Can you make it disappear?

Of course I can said Trong

And with a wave and a flash

There was just a puff of smoke

And a pile of smouldering ash

Have you enjoyed your visit Jack?

Yes it was simply great

And all you boys were very funny

There's nothing that I could hate

Do you think that I could come back again?

And visit you all at the fair

I don't know said Trong our time is so long

You might be eighty and lost all your hair

Maybe one day you'll come back to play

We can all have some fun once again

One night in a dream you'll see lots of steam

And you'll ride on a magical train

But we can never promise Jack

As I said we fairies die

So keep your friends believing in us

And bring you back I will try

Well said Trong I must take you home

But you will always be our friend

But for us Jack, it is getting late

And all good things come to an end

Jack went round and hugged all his mates

And said what a great time he'd had

I know I have to go home now

But to leave you I do feel sad

Jack you must take hold of my hand

And off they went in the sky

We will circle around and give a wave

Is that a tear I see in your eye?

Yes said Jack I must admit

I'm sorry to be leaving you all

I have had a wonderful time

In fact I've had a ball

Jack and Trong left the fair behind

Up in the dark night air

Past the park they heard a dog bark

Then down past an old broken chair

Trong took Jack high in the sky

And did a summersault then two

Round and round up and down

Past a cobweb covered with dew

Well said Trong there's your house

I'll take you back into your room

First I'll take you to the end of the road

And then we'll come back with a zoom

Jack and Trong flew through the window

And landed right on the bed

Right said Trong I must change you back

You may get a buzz in your head

Well thanks for saving me from the window sill

No thank you for a lovely time at the fair

Trong put out his hand to shake

And with a flash he wasn't there

Jack lay on his bed with a buzz in his head

As his mum walked through the door

It's dinner time Jack so get of your back

As I came in I heard you snore

Are you sure I was asleep said jack

I must have had dream I think

Never mind that said his mum

Your trainers do really stink

So jack went down for his dinner

And apologized for his actions that day

His dad said for being so good

Tomorrow you can go out to play

Jack returned to his bedroom

And didn't know if his journey was true

But on his bed was a rock piggy wig tail

With Trong written all the way through

Jack just smiled and picked up the tail

And laid on top of his bed

He tucked the tail under his pillow

And his eyes closed shut in his head

www.ingramcontent.com/pod-product-compliance
Lightning Source LLC
Chambersburg PA
CBHW061340040426
42444CB00011B/3021